Accelerated Reader

71725
The Globalization of Trade

Randall Frost
ATOS B.L: 10.6
ATOS Points: 2   UG

	382	Frost, Randall.
	FRO	The globalization of trade

DATE DUE	BORROWER'S NAME	ROOM NUMBER

382   Frost, Randall.

FRO   The globalization of trade

THE GLOBALIZATION OF TRADE

UNDERSTANDING GLOBAL ISSUES

Published by Smart Apple Media
1980 Lookout Drive
North Mankato, Minnesota 56003
USA

This book is based on *Fairer Global Trade?: The Challenge for the WTO*
Copyright ©1996 Understanding Global Issues Ltd., Cheltenham, England.

Library of Congress Cataloging-in-Publication Data

Frost, Randall.
 The globalization of trade / Randall Frost.
  p. cm. -- (Understanding global issues)
Summary: Explores the concept of trade in developed and undeveloped
countries, discussing the World Trade Organization, free trade versus
protectionism, and the environmental impacts of free trade.
Includes bibliographical references and index.
 ISBN 1-58340-363-9 (Library Bound : alk. paper)
 1. International trade--Juvenile literature. 2. World Trade
Organization. 3. Free trade--Social aspects--Juvenile literature. 4.
Free trade--Environmental aspects--Juvenile literature. 5.
Globalization--Juvenile literature. [1. International trade. 2. World
Trade Organization. 3. Free trade. 4. Globalization.] I. Title. II.
Series.
 HF1379.F765 2004
 382--dc21

                    2003000033

               Printed in Malaysia
               2 4 6 8 9 7 5 3 1

EDITOR Tina Schwartzenberger **COPY EDITOR** Heather Kissock
TEXT ADAPTATION Randall Frost **DESIGNER** Terry Paulhus
LAYOUT Katherine Phillips **PHOTO RESEARCHER** Wendy Cosh
SERIES EDITOR Jennifer Nault **CREATIVE COMPANY EDITOR** Jill Weingartz

Contents

Introduction

In early December 1999, representatives from more than 135 nations gathered in Seattle, Washington, for the World Trade Organization (WTO) Ministerial Conference. The conference, which meets at least once every two years, is the highest decision-making body in the WTO. At the top of the conference agenda was a new round of trade talks. The delegates' work was interrupted by a week of street protests and intermittent violence led by anti-**globalization** protesters who smashed store windows and stopped traffic.

In the end, the delegates' failure to launch their new round of **multilateral** trade negotiations took a back seat to the protests. As the media reported on the protests, many people around the world found themselves thinking for the first time about the role the global economy plays in their lives.

With the globalization of business, trade, and investment, the world is experimenting with **economic restructuring**. The hope is that this reshaping will produce better living standards for all, but as the anti-globalists

 Research has shown that countries that trade extensively with one another tend to experience greater overlaps in income levels.

point out, there is no guarantee that this will be the outcome. A world of rich elites and abounding poor is also possible. Indeed, this is already the reality in many parts of the globe.

Nearly half the world's population live on less than $2 per day.

World trade has become far larger and more complex than the United States and Great Britain could have imagined when they developed the original General Agreement on Tariffs and Trade (GATT) in 1947. Now, more than three-quarters of WTO members are from **developing countries** or former communist countries. More than 60 of these countries have introduced trade liberalization measures in recent years. While rich industrialized countries of the Organization for Economic Co-operation and Development (OECD) still dominate world trade, they no longer make all of the rules alone. The distinction between the rich North and poor South has become blurred as more and more developing countries build successful industrial economies.

The WTO, like the GATT that preceded it, commits its

members to helping developing countries. The Generalized System of Preferences, under which the poorest countries are granted special trade access conditions, has been given a permanent legal basis under the WTO. Still, inequality among the nations participating in the world trading system has increased. In spite of recent efforts to liberalize trade, there is little evidence that countries are approaching one another in terms of income levels. In fact, the income gaps between most countries appear to be increasing over time.

Trade liberalization since World War II has helped to lift billions of people out of poverty. However, nearly half the world's population, 2.8 billion people, live on less than $2 per day. The gap in living standards between rich and poor countries is now more than twice what it was 50 years ago.

Trade can lead to prosperity. In order to accomplish this it must operate fairly and distribute its benefits widely. Unrestricted **free trade** simply makes the rich richer by enabling them to strike unreasonable bargains with weaker trading partners. This is why there is a need for a set of international rules and a governing body to enforce them.

Trade Not War

In 2000, the value of world merchandise exports was $6.2 trillion, while world export of commercial services was valued at $1.4 trillion. Trade-related investment has also soared. Linking of the world's economies is well underway.

Trade between nations has grown rapidly as many developing countries and former communist states have embraced free markets, believing mutual trade should increase mutual wealth. Certainly, some Asian countries have successfully transformed living standards for their citizens through export-led growth and careful protection of key industries.

Child labor is widespread in developing countries because of poverty, an uneven distribution of wealth, and a wide range of societal and cultural norms.

Yet there is a trade-off. While global trade is growing rapidly, in many countries there is a mounting sense of job insecurity and increasing pressure on wages, labor conditions, and the environment. The link between economic and social development seems to have been broken, with income distribution continually becoming more skewed in favor of elites.

While most economic programs claim to bring developing countries into the global economy, the gap between rich and poor has widened. For example, in Mexico, which is

---

Some economic programs have widened the gap between rich and poor.

---

meant to benefit from the North American Free Trade Agreement (NAFTA), the richest 10 percent of wage earners earn as much as the bottom 70 percent. Such gross inequalities in income have a disruptive effect on societies.

Some theorists believe that if working people perceive the multilateral trade system as a threat, and not as an asset, a global system of economic governance must be developed to balance worldwide markets and add social dimension to international integration. Working men and women need confidence in the credibility of policies, as do the financial markets.

FREE TRADE VERSUS FAIR TRADE

Economists may differ in their assessments of the causes of and cures for international trade inequities, but they are basically in agreement that international trade and **foreign direct investment** (FDI) have been booming. For many people, however, the link between trade and prosperity is hard to see. There is growing unease over the impact of global free trade. **Fair trade** is a worthier and less divisive goal. It has yet to be determined whether global trade can be both fair and free.

The economic crisis in Mexico in the mid-1990s led to a serious decline in the standard of living and an increase in extreme poverty for most Mexicans.

Whereas the GATT was originally concerned with technical matters such as preventing countries from adopting protectionist measures, and customs duties, the WTO has been thrust into the debate on wider economic issues. Environmental protection, food safety, human rights, and labor rights are key concerns in the world trading system.

Aside from these issues, the WTO maintains a rules-based trading system that encourages fairness and openness among its more than 140 competitive trading nations. The habit of cheating or conducting negotiations outside the multilateral forum of the WTO is common. The WTO monitors international trade with a set of rules that ensures all traders play fair

and have the ability to resolve disputes without resorting to armed conflict.

Nations linked by trade and investment are unlikely to wage war with each other. The European community is the most obvious example of how economic ties can turn traditional enemies into trading partners, but it is unknown whether the same principle can apply on a global scale.

A world ungoverned by trade rules and dominated by the strong and ruthless—with no regard for social justice or the environment—would be an unpleasant place in which to live. Fortunately, the WTO provides a starting point for developing a fairer trading system.

COUNTRIES OUTSIDE OF THE WTO

Some countries in the Middle East and Africa, such as Iran, Iraq, and Zaire, remain outside of the WTO and have not applied for membership. North Korea has shown little interest in joining, but almost every other country in the world is either a WTO member or applicant. Approximately 30 countries are in various stages of accession—a complex process that can take several years. In addition, requests for admission have circulated from Syria and Libya. New members must make various commitments concerning national trade policy. Human rights, and social and environmental issues do not form part of WTO access negotiations.

Automobiles used to transport goods can emit harmful carbon dioxide which contributes to global warming.

New York City is the world's business and financial capital. It is the leading wholesale and retail trade center in the United States, largely because of its excellent port facilities and large population.

KEY CONCEPTS

The North American Free Trade Agreement (NAFTA) NAFTA was implemented on January 1, 1994, as a trade agreement between Mexico, Canada, and the United States. NAFTA removed most barriers to trade and investment among the three countries. The agreement also provides for environmental protection.

Tariff A tariff is a tax imposed on a product when it is imported into a country. Tariffs may be levied as a percentage of value or on a specific basis, such as a dollar amount per a specified weight. The purpose of tariffs is to provide a price advantage to similar locally produced merchandise and to raise government revenues.

Economist

Duties: Studies how society distributes resources such as land, labor, and raw materials to produce goods and services

Education: A graduate degree is required for most private sector economist jobs

Interests: The economy and how determining factors change it

Navigate to **www.inomics.com** for career information, or investigate the job outlook through the U.S. Department of Labor at **www.bls. gov/oco/ocos055.htm**.

Careers in Focus

Economists are concerned with economic theory and how it is applied in the world. They use mathematical models to help predict answers to economic questions. Economists conduct research, collect and analyze data, monitor economic trends, and develop economic forecasts.

There are many places that economists can work. They may be employed by insurance companies, banks, securities firms, industry and trade associations, labor unions, or governmental agencies. Economists prepare reports based on their findings in a clear and meaningful way.

An economist who works for the government may assess economic conditions in the United States or around the world, and estimate the economic effects of specific changes in public policy or legislation. He or she may also study the value of currency and its effect on imports and exports.

Other typical duties include planning and conducting surveys to collect economic data; analyzing and interpreting data; preparing reports; and briefing news media, industry, labor, and federal and state governments about economic trends. An economist may also be required to write articles and reports.

Graduate school offers economists the chance to specialize their focus. They may choose to study advanced economic theory, international economics, or labor economics.

Most economists have structured work schedules. They generally work alone, writing proposals, preparing charts, and using computers, but they are also an important part of research teams. Economists may also need to travel to fulfill their job requirements.

The Origins of the WTO

ollowing World War II, the international community shared a vision of a global community of democratic nations. This global community would be characterized by peaceful co-existence, economic development, and respect for human rights. It was to be closely linked to global institutions aimed at guaranteeing international security and economic order.

The 1940s gave birth to the GATT as a counterpart of the United Nations (UN), the **World Bank**, and the International Monetary Fund (IMF). The original intent was to set up an international trade organization as one of the pillars of the UN system. However, the U.S. Congress rejected this idea. For more than 40 years, the GATT remained a provisional set of international trading rules rather than a regulatory authority. The founders of the GATT had lived through the Great Depression. Memories of this gloomy period were reflected in the policies of the agreement. The economic crises and mass unemployment that had accompanied the protectionist world of the 1930s was thought to have contributed to World War II.

When the Cold War ended in the late 1980s, the vision of a new world order was revived. This time it seemed that almost every government worldwide shared the American dream of free markets. Even democracy and human rights seemed to be getting more attention.

This new world order created enough political will to support a stronger institutional framework for world trade. Under the terms of the Uruguay Round of GATT negotiations, the countries of the world finally agreed to set up the WTO. Membership in the WTO required acceptance of all the standards set out in the Uruguay Round. That meant committing to implement the Uruguay Round's 29 legal texts; 25 ministerial declarations, decisions, and understandings; and 24,000 pages of specific market access commitments.

Compared to just 23 signatories involved in the first GATT in 1947, the Uruguay Round saw talks between 115 countries—24 **developed countries** and 91 developing countries, including 24 of the poorest. By 2002, 144 countries belonged to the WTO.

Between 1950 and 2000, trade issues around the world changed. Reducing tariffs on manufactured goods remains central to the WTO. As well, negotiating agreements in other areas of international commerce, such as agriculture, basic telecommunications, services, **information technology**, **intellectual property**, and financial services, has increasingly become the focus of the WTO's agenda. Other concerns now include the impact of increasing trade.

In 1942, representatives of 26 nations met to sign the "Declaration of the United Nations." The first meeting of the General Assembly was held in Flushing Meadow, New York, in 1946.

AIMS OF THE WTO AGREEMENT

The introduction to the WTO Agreement sets positive goals for global living standards, full employment, sustainable development, and environmental protection. While the goals are worthy, it is questionable whether they are compatible with free trade. The agreement states:

When dealing with trade and economic endeavors an emphasis should be placed on improving and maintaining specific goals. These goals include improving living standards, and providing full employment with a growing amount of income and demand. Other goals focus on increasing the production and trade of goods and services while maintaining the best use of global resources with respect to sustainable development. Finding ways to protect and preserve the environment that are consistent with the varying levels of economic development is another goal.

Developing countries should be able to share in the growth of international trade. To meet this end, a framework must be created to ensure these countries receive secure compensation proportional to their economic development.

To aid these objectives, arrangements should benefit all parties. These arrangements are directed at reducing tariffs and trade barriers, as well as eliminating discriminatory treatment in international trade relations.

Using the GATT, past trade liberalization efforts, and the outcome of the Uruguay Round of Multilateral Trade Negotiations, a better system of multilateral trading will be created.

There is a need to uphold and continue to develop the basic standards of the multilateral trading system.

Once the WTO is in place, all parties must obey all GATT agreements.

The agreement to set up the WTO was a major achievement. It provides a framework on which a fair and orderly trading system can be built as long as member governments give it whole-hearted support. However, the short-term self-interest of some large nations and trading blocs, or nations that have common trading interests, could so dilute the power of the WTO as to make it ineffective.

The goal of the WTO is to facilitate "open, fair, and undistorted competition." The WTO is not a world government of trade that tells countries how they should shape policy. It is a **consensus**-based organization in which all member nations create a set of mutually beneficial rules for international trade. Rules are developed to provide maximum fairness, openness, and **transparency**. Within this broad framework, each nation inevitably struggles to advance its own interests, occasionally taking advantage of loopholes. Broadly speaking, the economic self-interest of nations is best served when playing by the rules. Some cheating occurs, but it may be restrained.

BASIC WTO PRINCIPLES

Non-discrimination
Every member of the WTO is expected to open its markets to every other party on equal terms, so that each shares in the benefits of the "most favored nation." This principle states that all WTO member nations have equal status and cannot discriminate against one another. When trading partners agree on a tariff cut, it is automatically extended to all other WTO members. Thus, smaller countries get the benefit of tariff cuts made by bigger countries without having to be involved in costly negotiations. The concept of national treatment means that a foreign-owned company operating in a member state has to be treated in the same way as a domestic company.

Predictable and growing access to markets
Countries belonging to the WTO agree to further open their markets. When countries negotiate a reduction in trade tariffs, they are encouraged to commit themselves to a tariff binding. In doing so, they promise not to unilaterally increase the tariff without providing compensation to their main trading partners. Tariff restrictions increase the stability of the world's trading environment.

Fair competition
Among the practices that can affect the fairness of trade competition are dumping, **subsidies**, and non-tariff barriers. Countries may introduce laws to protect health, safety, or the environment as long as such laws and standards do not act as barriers to trade and are applied equally both to domestic and foreign traders. As external tariffs have dropped, the monitoring of internal policies has become a more important aspect of WTO work.

Helping poorer countries
The WTO recognizes the need to help poorer countries and allows legislation that favors them through various measures such as the Generalized System of Preferences. For example, the WTO has a functioning system to help poor countries challenge discriminatory practices of stronger trading partners. An Advisory Center on WTO Law has been set up to help poor countries pursue cases under the Dispute Settlement Procedures. The Advisory center aims to help them exercise their rights on equal terms within the rules-based system. Developing countries are also given longer periods to implement WTO trade measures and are allowed to maintain higher tariffs on certain goods.

As a result, international cooperation remains as important as ever. Multilateral negotiations take the heat out of trading relationships between countries, enabling neutral discussion of problems. **Bilateral** negotiations, by contrast, can easily lead to political confrontation. The WTO contributes to world peace as well as economic order.

Fiberoptic communication systems allow vast quantities of information to be instantly transmitted across the globe.

CHOOSING A LEADER

After a long debate over who should be the first Director-General of the WTO, the member states agreed to appoint Italian lawyer and diplomat Renato Ruggiero. He took up his appointment on May 1, 1995, four months after the WTO began its official existence. Ruggiero was given a four-year tenure, and the United States insisted that his successor be non-European. Ruggiero was minister of foreign trade in the Italian government from 1987 to 1991. Mike Moore of New Zealand succeeded Ruggiero on September 1, 1999. Prior to becoming head of the WTO, Moore had served as New Zealand's Opposition Spokesperson on Foreign Affairs and Overseas Trade from 1993 to 1999. He also served as prime minister in 1990. As trade minister, Moore helped launch the Uruguay Round of GATT negotiations. He completed his term as Director-General on August 31, 2002. Moore's successor is Dr. Supachai Panitchpakdi, an economist from Thailand.

In recent decades, wheat, corn, and soybeans have become major foreign exchange commodities in the United States.

KEY CONCEPTS

Dumping Companies that export products at prices lower than the prices they normally charge on their own home market are said to be dumping the product. Dumping of low-priced goods on foreign markets is banned under WTO rules. Between 1995 and 2002, most WTO anti-dumping investigations have focused on China. Korea, the United States, Indonesia, and Japan have also been accused of numerous dumping violations.

International Monetary Fund (IMF) The IMF represents 184 member countries. It was established "to promote international monetary cooperation, exchange stability, and orderly exchange arrangements; to foster economic growth and high levels of employment; and to provide temporary financial assistance to countries to help ease balance of payments adjustment."

Non-tariff barriers Thanks to the GATT, tariffs on manufactured goods fell dramatically, from an average of about 40 percent in 1950 to below 5 percent in the mid-1990s. However, non-tariff measures became more prevalent as countries sought other ways to protect their domestic industries.

Examples include import quotas, voluntary import restraints, import licenses, "buy national" provisions, and other measures. Such measures include special labeling requirements and safety standards that go well beyond the protection of health and safety.

Uruguay Round The Uruguay Round of GATT negotiations started in 1986 and concluded in December 1993. It was by far the longest running and most ambitious of the eight rounds of international negotiations.

Biography
Dr. Supachai Panitchpakdi

Born: Bangkok, Thailand, in 1946
Education: Masters degree in Econometrics, Development Planning, and a Ph. D. in Economic Planning and Development from the Netherlands School of Economics
Legacy: Director-General of the WTO from 2002 to 2005

Navigate to the World Trade Organization's site **www.wto.org/ english/thewto_e/dg_e/dg_e. htm** to learn more about Dr. Panitchpakdi's role. Or, click on **www.us-asean.org/supachai.htm** to read his interview.

People in Focus

Dr. Supachai Panitchpakdi was elected Director-General of the World Trade Organization in September 1999. His three-year appointment started on September 1, 2002.

In 1974, Panitchpakdi began his professional career in the research department at the Bank of Thailand. While at the Bank of Thailand, he was a major force in devising measures to help troubled financial institutions in the 1980s. In 1986, he was appointed Deputy Minister of Finance. During his first term, he introduced a value-added tax system and helped devise strong policies that led to a series of budget surpluses. He was appointed Director and Advisor in 1988, and then president of the Thai Military Bank.

Panitchpakdi became Thailand's Deputy Prime Minister in 1992, supervising key economic offices.

In 1993, he helped convince the public and private sectors that Thailand needed to accept the Uruguay Round package. He represented Thailand at the signing of the Uruguay Round and has ensured Thailand's full and faithful implementation of their WTO obligations.

Panitchpakdi was the first to push for the formation of the Asia–Europe meeting. This assembly brings the heads of ruling powers in Asia and Europe together to create closer ties among the lawmaking units of the countries. He has also pushed for economic integration among the economies of China, Laos, Thailand, Cambodia, Myanmar, and Vietnam.

Panitchpakdi was appointed Thailand's Deputy Prime Minister and Minister of Commerce in 1997. He relaxed Thailand's restrictions on foreign participation and ownership. He also brought accounting standards in line with international practices.

How the WTO Works

The core tasks of the WTO are to help trade flow as freely as possible, to ensure that individuals, companies, and governments know what the trade rules are around the world, and to settle trade disputes. Therefore, the WTO administers and enforces the multilateral and **plurilateral** trade agreements that together make up the WTO treaty. It also acts as a forum for multilateral trade negotiations, oversees national trade policies, and cooperates with other international institutions to develop reasonable policies for the world economy. The WTO engages the representatives of more than 140 countries in a continuous series of trade negotiations. The "most favored nation" principle ensures that agreements are extended to all WTO members. While tariffs and protectionist measures are allowed, lowering all barriers to international trade is encouraged. However, many

WTO director Mike Moore; Qatari Minister of Finance, Economy, and Trade, Youssef Hussain Kamal; and China's Foreign Trade Minister, Shi Guangheng, toasted China's new WTO membership in Doha in 2001.

barriers remain in place, and practices that go against the spirit of the WTO Agreement are sometimes ignored.

Without the WTO's set of international trading rules, a confusing number of bilateral agreements would create a kind of **anarchy**. This would be far worse for weaker countries than the current regime. While the stronger trading nations may retain the upper hand, at least they agree to abide by certain rules of conduct. Far from being a tool of the big countries, the WTO can be a guardian of the weak.

The credibility of the world trading system depends on the goodwill of WTO members to enforce the agreed-upon rules. However, some have argued

> *The credibility of the world trading system depends on the goodwill of WTO members to enforce the agreed-upon rules.*

that enforcement is not suitable for the trade of public goods—first, because the member states will not put up with it, and second, because many countries are too poor to put international standards in place. In any case,

leaning on small developing countries is one thing, but forcing the United States or the European Union (EU) to toe the line is quite a different matter. It is uncertain whether the WTO can really ensure that the biggest trading nations abide by both the spirit and the letter of world trading laws. Perhaps giving the WTO more political power to enforce the will of the majority is an option worth considering.

The WTO, the International Monetary Fund (IMF), and the World Bank enjoy equal standing. Voting is unweighted only in the WTO, where each member nation gets one vote.

THE THREE STAGES OF SETTLING DISPUTES: CONSULTATION, PANEL REPORT, AND APPEAL

The WTO, besides providing a secure set of rules for fair and open global trade, broke important ground by offering an effective way to settle trade disputes between member states. The WTO is better equipped to settle trade disputes than the GATT was. When a member state believes a trading partner is breaking WTO rules and harming trade, it may seek recourse through the Dispute Settlement Body (DSB) of the WTO's General Council. If consultations fail to produce a solution within 60 days, the country bringing the dispute can ask the DSB to set up a panel to study the case in detail. The panel has to provide its final report to the two sides within six months, or three months if perishable goods are involved. Three weeks after this, the report is circulated to all WTO members. The report becomes the DSB's ruling or recommendation within 60 days, unless a consensus rejects it. Either party may appeal to a standing Appellate Body comprising seven independent experts. Appeal proceedings take no more than 60 to 90 days, after which the DSB must accept or reject its report within 30 days. Rejection is only possible by consensus. The appeal findings then become binding. Even if the dispute goes to appeal, settlement should not take more than 15 months at most. Under the GATT, disputes often lasted for many years.

In June 2000, trade representatives from the United States told the U.S. Senate Finance Committee that the WTO's dispute settlement mechanism had "proven itself, after five years of experience, to have changed the world trade environment for the better." In just seven years, the WTO had handled nearly 250 cases. In contrast, only 300 disputes were dealt with during the entire 47-year life of GATT. Among the causes of complaint to the WTO have been Argentinean taxes on imported textiles, Canadian subsidies of exported dairy products, Indian import bans, Japanese restrictions on imported fruit, and U.S. import restrictions on conventional and reformulated gasoline.

CASE STUDY: U.S. VERSUS VENEZUELA

In January 1995, Venezuela lodged a complaint with the DSB against the United States. Venezuela asserted that the United States applied stricter rules on the chemical composition of imported gasoline than it did on domestically refined gasoline. Venezuela, later joined by Brazil, argued that the U.S. trade barrier was unfair because U.S. gasoline refiners did not have to meet the same requirements. This violated the WTO's national treatment principle. In April 1995, the DSB sided with Venezuela and Brazil. The decision was upheld in an appeal report. The United States subsequently agreed to amend its regulations within 15 months. In August 1997, the U.S. reported to the DSB that a new regulation had been enacted.

The U.S. and a small country such as Burundi thus have equal voting power. The WTO has been likened to a club whose members set rules of conduct for trading operations between themselves. Peer group pressure, rather than legal restrictions, is what keeps members in line. Sometimes members may choose to ignore violations of the rules, especially if one of the big trading nations is involved. The WTO is only as powerful as its larger members allow it to be.

Almost all merchandise trade and agricultural products, plus certain services and intellectual property, are covered by the WTO Agreement. Some member countries have signed separate agreements on liberalization of financial services. In July 2002, the United States announced its own set of proposals for liberalizing global trade in financial services, including banking and insurance.

As in the GATT, decision-making in the WTO seeks consensus. Decisions can be made by a majority vote in some cases. To adopt an interpretation of a multilateral trade agreement or waive obligations imposed on a particular member state, a three-quarters majority is needed. A two-thirds majority is required to admit new WTO members or amend certain provisions of a WTO trade agreement. Major changes still need the backing of all member states.

Each member of the EU has one vote, though negotiations on trade policies are delegated to the European Commission, with the Trade Commissioner acting as head of the negotiating team. The U.S., Canada, Japan, and the EU are the most important WTO influences, with Brazil, India, and South Africa among the leaders of developing country interests. Russia is not yet a WTO member, but will likely be admitted. Without Russia, the WTO cannot truly represent global trade.

The member states' governments, influenced by lobby groups representing business organizations, labor unions, farmers, and consumer groups, set the members' trade policies and negotiating positions. Transnational companies (TNCs) are among the most active and powerful

According to the United States Department of Energy (DOE), the United States imports 9,328,000 barrels of crude oil each day. Saudi Arabia is the top supplier of crude oil to the United States.

groups lobbying the WTO. In the mid-1990s, about one-third of all international trade consisted of intracompany imports and exports, as TNCs transferred components and profits between different factories in different parts of the world.

Under its constitution, the WTO has a responsibility to help developing countries and countries in transition to free-market economies. To aid this effort, the WTO Training Institute opened in June 2001. The institute offers introductory courses on the WTO to the least-developed countries, courses on dispute-settlement rules and procedures, and courses for delegates and WTO staff members who have recently arrived in Geneva, Switzerland, where the WTO is located.

STRUCTURE OF THE WTO

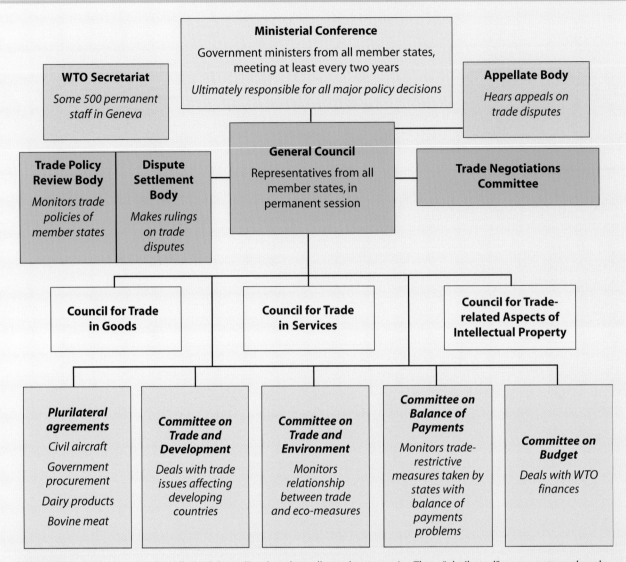

Ministerial Conference

Government ministers from all member states, meeting at least every two years

Ultimately responsible for all major policy decisions

WTO Secretariat

Some 500 permanent staff in Geneva

Appellate Body

Hears appeals on trade disputes

Trade Policy Review Body

Monitors trade policies of member states

Dispute Settlement Body

Makes rulings on trade disputes

General Council

Representatives from all member states, in permanent session

Trade Negotiations Committee

Council for Trade in Goods

Council for Trade in Services

Council for Trade-related Aspects of Intellectual Property

Plurilateral agreements

Civil aircraft

Government procurement

Dairy products

Bovine meat

Committee on Trade and Development

Deals with trade issues affecting developing countries

Committee on Trade and Environment

Monitors relationship between trade and eco-measures

Committee on Balance of Payments

Monitors trade-restrictive measures taken by states with balance of payments problems

Committee on Budget

Deals with WTO finances

Note: WTO agreements are normally "multilateral" and apply to all member countries. These "plurilateral" agreements apply only to certain members.

KEY CONCEPTS

European Union (EU) The EU is the organization of European countries. The organization works to increase economic integration and strengthen cooperation among its members. The EU has 15 member states and is preparing for the admission of 13 additional eastern and southern European countries.

Transnational company (TNC) A TNC is a business that manages foreign direct investments (FDIs) and produces goods or services in more than one country. TNCs are important global players and have considerable resources. These companies are becoming increasingly virtual, or less tied to one country.

Duties: Convinces government officials to take the lobbyist's stance on certain issues
Education: No specific education is required, but legal training is helpful
Interests: Politics, an interest in particular groups or organizations

Navigate to **www.lobbyist.org** to learn more about how to become a lobbyist and link to career opportunities. Also click on **www.alldc.org** for more information about lobbying as a profession.

Careers in Focus

While no specific training is required to become a lobbyist, succeeding in the profession does depend on an individual's experience. People who choose to become lobbyists have varying experience, such as training in law, teaching, public relations, and journalism. A successful lobbyist must have political experience and understand how the political system works. Possibly the best place to train and learn lobbying is in a congressional office. This helps the lobbyist gain experience with the legislative process, and allows him or her to develop close ties with the people involved in making important decisions.

To begin a career as a lobbyist, one must choose an organization to lobby for. The organization should be one that shares the lobbyist's beliefs and values, rather than one that the lobbyist does not believe in.

It is helpful, but not necessary, for the lobbyist to have some kind of experience with the organization before becoming a lobbyist for it. The lobbyist must then become an expert on his or her chosen cause or organization. This is an essential part of being a lobbyist. It is very important that the lobbyist understands his or her client's interests and the laws and policies he or she hopes to influence. Because of this, the lobbyist must be able to communicate effectively both in writing and speaking.

A lobbyist can work at either the state or federal level. Legislation tends to move faster at the state level because of its smaller size.

Global Investment, Global Trade

In recent years, international trade has been increasing at more than twice the world's combined **gross domestic product** (GDP). However, an economic downturn that began in early 2001, and which was intensified by the September 11 terrorist attacks in the U.S., left widespread devastation in world economies. East Asia and Latin America took the hardest hits.

Foreign direct investment (FDI) has been growing faster than international trade in recent years and has exceeded domestic investment in many developing countries. Improvements in transport and communications have made it far easier to sell goods and services around the world. Real transport costs today are one-quarter of what they were in the 1920s.

Until the 2001 economic downturn, global trade, at 12 percent, was growing at more than twice the rate of global output, at 4.5 percent, speeding linkage of the world economy. The main beneficiaries of global free trade have been financial markets and TNCs of industrial countries, with shareholders and consumers also standing to gain. This does not necessarily mean that the persistence of global poverty has proven that the world trading system is unfair. It does suggest that there may be a way to more evenly distribute the benefits of trade.

There is no way that the globalization of business, trade, and investment can be reversed. Globalization has come to mean that investors in Hong Kong buy and sell companies in London. Globalization means that products made partly in the U.S. and partly in Poland are

■ **Some transnational companies (TNCs) have been accused of moving operations from country to country to take advantage of low labor costs, low taxes, and lack of regulations.**

REGIONAL TRADING BLOCS

Regional trading arrangements are allowed under WTO rules—as long as countries do not set up barriers to non-members. Some of the principal trading blocs are:

European Union (EU) The EU is the largest, and by far the most closely integrated, trading bloc. The EU operates a customs union and a single market with, in theory, complete freedom of movement of goods, services, capital, and people. The trading bloc imposes a wide range of social and environmental measures. Monetary union is also part of the trade strategy. It is designed to protect national currencies from attack by speculators and to preclude competitive devaluations that give unfair trading advantages by suddenly making the exports of a country cheaper. It is hoped that the changeover of EU currency to the Euro will have a dynamic effect on intra-EU trade, which already accounts for more than half of member states' imports and exports.

North American Free Trade Agreement (NAFTA) Links the economies of Canada, Mexico, and the U.S., and liberalizes trade between them.

Mercosur A free trade region involving Argentina, Brazil, Paraguay, Uruguay, Chile, and Bolivia. Mercosur hopes to incorporate all South American countries by 2005.

The Association of Southeast Asian Nations (ASEAN) Thailand, Brunei Darussalam, Cambodia, Laos, Burma, Vietnam, Malaysia, Indonesia, Myanmar, Singapore, and the Republic of the Philippines have agreed to develop a free trade area. The 21 members of the Asia Pacific Economic Co-operation group (APEC), which include Australia, Brunei Darussalam, Canada, Chile, People's Republic of China (China), Hong Kong (China), Indonesia, Japan, Republic of Korea (South Korea), Malaysia, Mexico, New Zealand, Papua New Guinea, Peru, the Republic of the Philippines, Russia, Singapore, Chinese Taipei (Taiwan), Thailand, the United States, and Vietnam, have also agreed on ASEAN aims to accelerate economic growth, social progress, and cultural development while also promoting peace and stability.

Although most developing countries are members of regional trade organizations, they are not members of the major trade organizations such as the EU and NAFTA, which encompass major export markets. The question for the future is whether regional free trade areas will serve to complement the global system, reinforcing the move towards open trade, or if they will evolve into protected, "fortress-style" trading blocs.

sold in Brazil, and that jobs in Canada are affected by wage rates in Mexico. Today, consumers everywhere have become used to buying products from different countries.

The motor vehicle industry provides a good example of how globalization has affected trading and investment patterns. A Mercedes-Benz truck, for instance, may be assembled in Indonesia, its engine made in Brazil, its drive train made in India, and its power-steering made in Japan. Trade between nations is essential to human health, prosperity, and social welfare. Many of the goods and services that sustain our lives, including the foods that we eat, depend on foreign trade.

Globalization, with all its competitive pressures, is a mixed blessing. Perhaps those who deal in finance get the most out of globalization. They can take advantage of the freedom to place money wherever it produces the highest return.

In theory, the globalization of business should bring consumers improved choice, quality, and prices. Still, consumers are just as interested in quality of life and job security as they are in well-stocked supermarket shelves.

Electronic money transfers can make the movement of money swift and hard to trace, maximizing profit and making tax collection difficult. From $1.2 to $2 trillion per day is estimated to move in and out of the world's financial markets. Most of this investment is speculative and has nothing to do with the real economy—providing little capital for agriculture, manufacturing, or service industries.

International trade in finance and securities has a long history, but the scale and freedom of money movements in today's markets have largely outreached the regulatory capacity of national governments. As financial crises in Southeast Asia, Russia, and Mexico have

Globalization is bringing a level of economic mobility that has the potential to be extremely disruptive to human lives.

demonstrated, when currency speculators rapidly pull out their funds, the human cost can be enormous. Eventually, international regulation and even taxation may provide an answer, but such reforms will be very hard to put in place. Although these issues are not yet on the WTO's official agenda, anti-globalization activists continue to lobby the WTO for just such a tax on the global currency market. The United Nations issued a January 2001 report on "currency transaction taxes" that could finance social development and poverty eradication programs around the world.

Competition among TNCs is often brutal. Investment decisions about operating in a foreign country are not taken lightly. Labor costs are only part of the calculation, but following the adoption of NAFTA, many

U.S. companies moved assembly operations to Mexico, cutting labor costs from about $12 per hour to $1 or $2 per hour. Despite political and economic uncertainties in Mexico, the average annual inflow of foreign direct investment to that country was $11.8 billion between 1994 and 1999. In addition, some U.S. companies have moved to Canada, where assembly costs are 20 to 25 percent below those in the U.S.

Although it often makes good business sense for a TNC to move to a lower-cost production area, companies must be careful not to damage their image. Customers do not like greedy and irresponsible corporate behavior—if they find out about it. There are even reports of companies who are threatening to move to Mexico as a way to drive down wages in the U.S. or to impose tougher working conditions on the labor force.

It is far easier for products and money to flow between countries than it is for people to move. International mobility of labor is largely confined to highly paid executives and a handful of people with special skills. While migrant labor is an important factor in some job markets, most people cannot simply uproot themselves and their families to follow job opportunities around the world. Globalization is bringing a level of economic mobility that has the potential to be extremely disruptive to human lives.

The common market program in the EU includes broad social aims. Once-poor countries such as Spain, Portugal, Ireland, and Greece have benefited greatly from EU membership. For example, they have obtained regional grants and human rights improvements, while also securing market access for their goods. NAFTA, however, is almost exclusively a free trade agreement. Anti-globalization activists argue that the pressure to lower wages in the U.S. and Canada, and environmental and social deterioration in Mexico, have shown that free-market forces do not necessarily improve people's lives—at least in the short term. This may, however, change over time.

Globalization makes measures directed at social equity and improvement more important, but also more difficult to implement.

EXPORT PROCESSING ZONES

Many global companies do not actually manufacture anything—they put their brand labels on merchandise purchased from overseas export processing zones. These zones are most frequently located in developing countries, such as Indonesia, China, Mexico, Vietnam, and the Philippines. The companies are typically offered lengthy tax-free periods in exchange for agreeing to do business in the zones. There may also be few restrictions on sending profits and foreign exchange back to the home country.

International companies operating in export processing zones hire workers in the manufacturing plants they contract with, as do local businesses that support the manufacturing activities. Most of the workers in the zones are women between the ages of 16 and 25, and most are employed as production workers.

Wages in the zones tend to be low compared to more formal sectors of the local economies such as manufacturing, and some workers find that they barely make enough to live on. Although there are no laws against forming labor unions in the zones, in some countries, government authorization has been required before employees can form a union.

It has been argued that these zones provide opportunities for developing countries to acquire new technologies, leading to greater employment. However, most workers in the zones are engaged in unskilled and semi-skilled labor. As a result, technology transfer tends to be limited to the skills acquired in particular production processes.

One possible outcome of this tension would be the EU maintaining external barriers to protect its home-grown industries, jobs, and living standards. Other regional fortresses could develop. So far, the increasing trade within regional blocs such as Asia-Pacific, NAFTA, and the EU has been complemented by wider trade with partners in other regions. Nevertheless, the temptation to lock into protectionist groups is strong.

In a global free market, high-wage economies must compete with low-wage economies. High-wage economies clearly cannot offer low labor costs and must concentrate on other factors, such as technology and knowledge. Finding jobs for the unskilled becomes a new problem. It is an issue that goes to the heart of modern politics.

During the rise of globalization, big business has increasingly operated without the control of national governments. Globalization has

Supplemental agreements to NAFTA addressed concerns that production plants in the U.S. would move operations to Mexico to take advantage of cheaper labor.

also undermined the ability of governments to protect the interests of their citizens by laying down certain social and environmental standards. The hope is that bodies such as the WTO can shape new international agreements that will help to spread codes of best practice around the world.

KEY CONCEPTS

Trading bloc A trade or trading bloc is a group of countries who join together to promote trade among themselves. Customs procedures and external tariffs are usually the same within the bloc. Member nations usually trade freely between themselves, without any tariffs. Trading blocs aim to establish common markets, promoting harmonious and balanced development of economic activities and closer relations among member states. The main purpose of a trading bloc, however, is to strengthen negotiation with external parties.

Born: June 5, 1723, in Kirkcaldy, Scotland
Education: Studied at the University of Glasgow and Oxford University
Legacy: Founding father of modern economics; author of *The Wealth of Nations*

Navigate to **www.econlib.org/ library/Enc/bios/Smith.html** or **www.acton.org/research/ libtrad/smith.html** to learn more about Adam Smith.

People in Focus

Adam Smith has been called the founding father of modern economics. His best-known work was *The Wealth of Nations*. Published in 1776, the book addresses the benefits of and the need for division of labor or specialization and the workings of the price system. Many of Smith's ideas are standard economic theories today.

Smith graduated from the University of Glasgow at the age of 17. He went on to hold a fellowship at Oxford University before returning to Scotland, where he lectured at Edinburgh and Glasgow universities.

After leaving the University of Glasgow, he traveled and visited some of the most influential thinkers of his time. His time away from the university gave him an opportunity to work through his theories. When he returned to

Scotland, he began work on *The Wealth of Nations*. Smith argued in his writings that market forces lead to the production of the right goods and services because producers are motivated to make profits by providing them. In a free-market economy without government intervention, Smith said, the well-being of the public would increase as a result of market competition.

Smith believed that labor was both the source and the final measure of value. Wages depended on the basic needs of workers, and rent depended on the productivity of land. Profits were the difference between selling prices and the costs of labor and rent. According to Smith, profits would be used to expand production. This would create more jobs, and the national income would grow.

Adam Smith was critical of trade tariffs. He believed free trade and a self-regulating economy would result in social progress. Smith's beliefs that the government should not interfere in business policies and his analysis of economic forces formed the basic ideas of economic liberalism.

Mapping WTO Membership

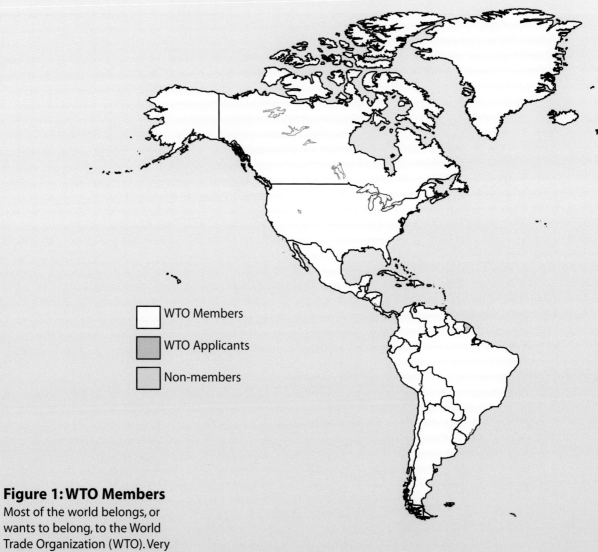

WTO Members

WTO Applicants

Non-members

Figure 1: WTO Members

Most of the world belongs, or wants to belong, to the World Trade Organization (WTO). Very few countries are non-members. Several countries are in various stages of the application process.

Scale 1:140,000,000

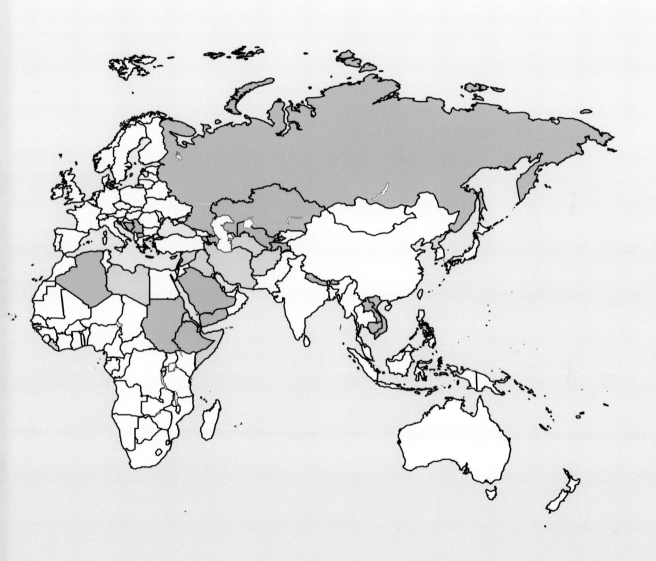

Charting Global Trade

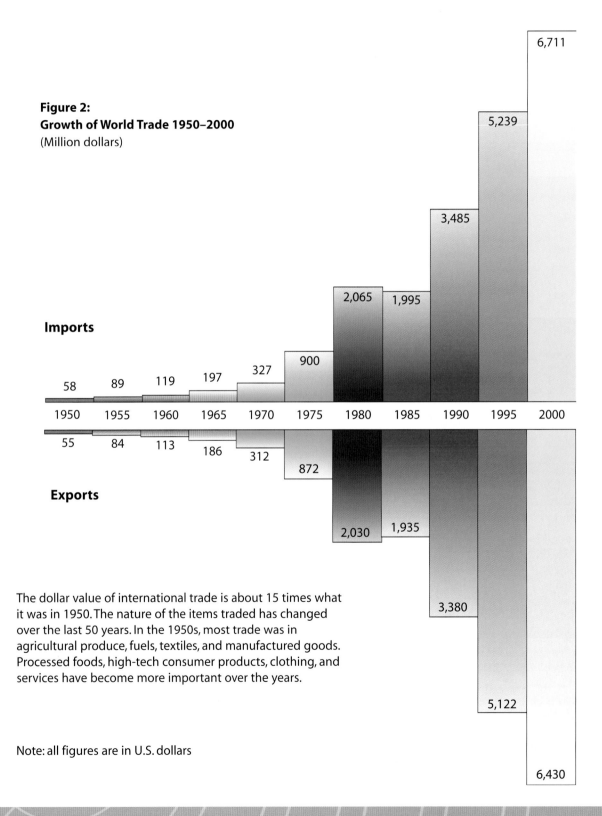

Figure 2:
Growth of World Trade 1950–2000
(Million dollars)

Imports

1950	1955	1960	1965	1970	1975	1980	1985	1990	1995	2000
58	89	119	197	327	900	2,065	1,995	3,485	5,239	6,711

Exports

1950	1955	1960	1965	1970	1975	1980	1985	1990	1995	2000
55	84	113	186	312	872	2,030	1,935	3,380	5,122	6,430

The dollar value of international trade is about 15 times what it was in 1950. The nature of the items traded has changed over the last 50 years. In the 1950s, most trade was in agricultural produce, fuels, textiles, and manufactured goods. Processed foods, high-tech consumer products, clothing, and services have become more important over the years.

Note: all figures are in U.S. dollars

Figure 3:
Leading exporters and importers in world trade in commercial services, 2001
(Billion dollars)

Country	Import	Export
United States	187.7	263.4
United Kingdom	91.6	108.4
France	61.6	79.8
Germany	132.6	79.7
Japan	107	63.7
Spain	33.2	57.4
Italy	55.7	57
The Netherlands	52.9	51.7
Belgium-Luxembourg	39.3	42.6
Hong Kong	25.1	42.4
Canada	41.5	35.6
China	39	32.9

Figure 4:
Leading exporters and importers in world trade in merchandise trade, 2001
(Billion dollars)

Country	Import	Export
United States	1180.2	730.8
Germany	492.8	570.8
Japan	349.1	403.5
France	325.8	321.8
United Kingdom	331.8	273.1
China	243.6	266.2
Canada	227.2	259.9
Italy	232.9	241.1
The Netherlands	207.3	229.5
Hong Kong	202	191.1

For the most part, the world's leading importers and exporters are the same for trade in commercial services and merchandise trade. However, their placement in the top ten changes significantly between the two.

Figure 5:
Merchandise Trading Partners with the U.S., 2001
(Billion dollars)

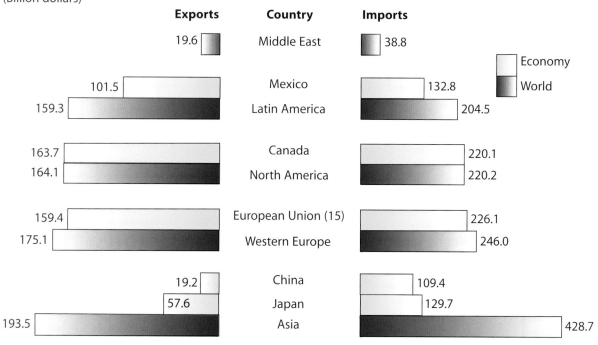

This graph shows the largest trading partners of the United States. Most countries that the U.S. exports goods to are the same countries from whom the U.S. imports goods.

Free Trade versus Protectionism

Although some financial markets come close to the free trade ideal, genuine free trade probably exists more in textbooks than in real life. Even countries with open markets manage trade in various ways. Subsidies, technical standards, tax incentives, and regulations may all operate as disguised forms of trade **protectionism**.

There is is a common misperception that the WTO advocates global free trade. Total reliance on free-market forces would soon result in a mercantile free-for-all dominated by bullies because the strong and the efficient stand to gain the most under these conditions. The question to ask is how much regulation and government interference is needed to make the international trading system operate openly, fairly, and efficiently for the mutual benefit of all those who participate. Getting the right balance between open markets and safeguards is extremely difficult, especially when each country is trying to advance its own trading interests.

The WTO frequently has difficulty achieving consensus on proposals for reform because member states are free to negotiate from their own self-interests. As WTO membership grows, it seems inevitable that future discussions will encounter even more problems. In the past, GATT negotiators took a relatively narrow, technical view of their role. The public expects the WTO to address much broader and more political issues, including policing the flow of money and using trade to advance social and environmental goals.

However, many feel that the WTO is poorly qualified to deal with complex and highly charged issues such as environmental protection, food safety, human and labor rights, except as they relate to international trade. This is because of the organization's lack of credibility and expertise in these areas. To date, the WTO has only become involved in such issues with an eye toward preventing them from being used for protectionist purposes.

The battle lines in the disputes about social and environmental measures are clearly drawn. Advocates of maximum trade liberalization are led by TNCs seeking to optimize their global profits on behalf of shareholders. On the opposing side are labor unions, anxious to prevent foreign imports from destroying their members' jobs, and pressure groups, concerned about environmental destruction or unequal distribution of global wealth. Politicians trying to exert complete control over their national economies are also among the opponents to maximum trade liberalization.

Vancouver, British Columbia, Canada, is one of North America's busiest ports. Vancouver's leading trading partners are Brazil, China, Japan, Taiwan, and the U.S.

At the government level, almost all administrations around the world are embracing free-market capitalism, aiming for open markets, monetary stability, deregulation, and privatization.

By the mid-1990s, the international debt crisis and the collapse of communism had resulted in more than 60 developing countries changing their economic policies from protectionism to liberalization. These countries have accepted economic programs to stabilize their finances, welcomed foreign investment, and slashed tariff barriers. In some Latin American and African countries, however, the immediate result of these policies has been an increase in poverty and suffering among already disadvantaged people. People have argued that the governing elites' enthusiasm for open markets stems more from new opportunities for personal gain than from a desire to benefit the economy as a whole. Bribery and corruption have been common features of the rush toward free markets in both the developing world and the former communist countries.

Bribery and corruption have been common features of the rush toward free markets.

World Bank economists predicted that the more open markets and lower tariffs of the Uruguay Round would yield an extra $200 billion per year in global income, but the Uruguay Round produced nothing resembling free trade. Many barriers remain in place. Although agriculture was brought into the GATT for the first time, dirty tariffication was used to keep barriers in place by raising the base tariff on which the agreed reductions were to be made. Subsidies have ensured that the domestic consumers of Japanese rice and Swiss butter continue to pay several times the world market price.

In addition, as critics have pointed out, the removal of tariff and non-tariff restrictions on agricultural products, textiles, and shoes is often phased out over a much longer period than on advanced industrial goods. The abolition of the Multifibre Arrangement is currently phasing out tariffs on textiles over a 10-year period. Safeguard measures can still be invoked if a country feels it is being hurt by imports. GATT covered fewer than half of the service sectors in most of the Organization for Economic Co-operation and Development (OECD) countries,

THE CASE FOR OPEN TRADE

"The economic case for an open trading system based upon multilaterally agreed rules is simple enough and rests largely on commercial common sense … liberal trade policies—policies that allow the unrestricted flow of goods and services—multiply the rewards that result from producing the best products, with the best design, at the best price. But success in trade is not static. The ability to compete well in particular products can shift from company to company when the market changes or new technologies make cheaper and better products possible … When the trading system is allowed to operate without the constraints of protectionism, firms are encouraged to adapt gradually and in a relatively painless way … The alternative is protection against competition from imports, and perpetual government subsidies. That leads to bloated, inefficient companies supplying consumers with outdated, unattractive products. Ultimately, factories close and jobs are lost despite the protection and subsidies. If other governments around the world pursue the same policies, markets contract and world economic activity is reduced. One of the objectives of the WTO is to prevent such a self-defeating and destructive drift into protectionism."

From the WTO's official brochure *Trading into the Future*

and less than 20 percent in most developing countries.

Conventional economic theorists continue to see open trade as the foundation of wealth. However, unemployment in the rich world and continuing poverty in the developing world, especially in Latin America and Africa, have contributed to doubts about the benefits of global free trade. Japan's economy thrived throughout the 1980s despite its protected market, and the East Asian "miracle" economies have combined their emphasis on exports with carefully judged protection of key industries. Asia's success does not support the benefits of either free trade or protectionism.

The Uruguay Round, whatever its overall failures or accomplishments, set in place a better and more open system covering a wider range of traded goods and services. It also reduced the effect of tariff escalation and the higher customs duties on processed goods imposed by rich countries. This form of protectionism has interfered with attempts made by poor countries to sell commodities to the much more profitable business of food processing

██████ **Living conditions in many underdeveloped countries are crude, and opportunities for children to get an education are limited. Many families lack basic necessities of life, such as shelter, adequate food, and clean water.**

or manufacturing. However, many poor countries have still experienced declining trade in manufactured goods.

Still, policy makers insist that in the end, free trade will make everyone richer. They argue that there is no alternative to the "compete or die" law of

nature. What no one knows is how much protection is needed to soften the impact of open markets on the most vulnerable citizens and to make trade fair and open.

Social and Green Issues

Even before the 1999 protests at the Seattle Ministerial Conference, concerned individuals and organizations, aside from environmentalists and trade unions, had become concerned about the impact of global free trade. International trade union organizations were demanding that a social clause be built into trade agreements. They wanted a ban on forced labor and child labor, guaranteed freedom of association and the right to organize and bargain collectively, rules to ensure a safe and healthy workplace, non-discrimination in employment, and appropriate standards concerning hours of work.

The *maquiladoras*, or "sweatshop workers," of Latin America have some of the worst labor and environmental conditions in the world. Of the million or so *maquiladoras* in Mexico, many are girls and young women between the ages of 14 and 20. They work 6 days per week in grueling 10-hour shifts with few breaks. Working conditions are usually hazardous, and industrial accidents and exposures to toxic chemicals are common. On average, *maquiladoras* earn between $0.80 and $1.25 per hour. It is difficult to know if global free trade will replicate such horrors across the world or will bring increased incomes and new awareness of

Tens of thousands of concerned citizens were drawn to the 1999 WTO protests in Seattle.

workers' rights. Much will depend on the international agreements hammered out in the WTO.

Global free trade is a two-edged sword. On the one hand, it provides new opportunities for business, but it also increases competitive pressures. To prevent a downward spiral of wages and working conditions, some have advocated that a minimum code of labor standards be built into WTO trade agreements.

Improving environmental standards has been of as much concern as social issues. Exporting toxic waste is perhaps the most blatant way in which "green" standards in rich countries can damage the environment in poor countries, but developing countries cannot afford to impose the rigorous anti-pollution measures that German or U.S. citizens have come to expect from their industries.

Some have advocated that a minimum code of labor standards be built into WTO agreements.

WTO rules do not prevent a country from regulating trade in certain products in order to protect health or the environment. However, the country cannot use such measures as protectionist devices and must apply the rules equally to both domestic and foreign suppliers. One country cannot impose its law on another's production processes.

Measures to protect the environment can sometimes act as constraints on trade, yet action is urgently needed to counteract the damaging effects of some types of trade on the environment. Examples include threats to the ozone layer caused by greenhouse gases, transport of hazardous materials across international borders, and trade in endangered species. Most merchandise trade increases pressure on the environment through transport, packaging, and waste. On the other hand, trade can increase wealth and quality of life. A balanced approach must be put into practice.

CHILD LABOR AND GLOBAL FREE TRADE

The minimum working age set in the International Labor Organization's (ILO) Convention on Child Labor is 15, although in special circumstances it may be 14. Yet in 2000, the ILO estimated that there were 211 million children between the ages of 5 and 14 working around the world. This equates to just under one-fifth of all children in this age group. Of these children, about 73 million were younger than 10 years old. This seems like exploitation of the worst kind—and it often is.

Compared to the WTO, the ILO is almost without power, prompting critics of globalization to argue for a greater role for the WTO in enforcing labor standards. Many labor violations have nothing to do with international trade and may have no impact on it. In many countries, for example, child labor is not seen as exploitation but as a normal part of family life. Children work alongside their parents and other relatives in extended family businesses. Others, less fortunate, work in factories, fields, or mines.

Some have argued for greater ratification and enforcement of ILO conventions. Although a worldwide legal ban on child labor might sound like a good idea, it could actually make matters worse, further driving struggling families into poverty. A recent agreement negotiated in Brazil suggests a possible solution. There, a successful pilot project pays subsidies to poor families if all the children in the family regularly attend school. A more recent proposal would reward girls with a savings account if they complete eight years of school.

In 1991, prior to the establishment of the WTO, a GATT panel report prohibited the U.S. from imposing its own requirements for the dolphin-friendly fishing of tuna on Mexican boats that used catch-all nets. The report was never adopted, and Mexico and the United States held their own bilateral consultations aimed at reaching agreement outside the GATT, but maintaining the distinction gave the GATT a bad name with environmentalists.

A more recent case involved a U.S. regulation that banned the importing of shrimp caught with methods that did not protect endangered turtles. The regulation was challenged in the WTO. In June 2001, a WTO panel upheld the U.S. ban, noting that the U.S. had made attempts to negotiate a turtle protection treaty. This ruling was an important victory for environmentalists, and set a precedent that could be used in other environmental cases.

A former United States trade representative acknowledged in October 1999 that the United States has not relaxed any environmental, health, or safety law to comply with any WTO ruling, even though several of the cases were lost by the U.S. The representative went on to explain that changes to U.S. laws have been made only to remove discrimination in the treatment of foreign and U.S. companies.

The WTO continues to argue that social and environmental matters are best left out of trade negotiations and should be put in separate international agreements. Trade can be a powerful tool for change. Whether the WTO likes it or not, trade has moved to the front line in the battle against environmental degradation and social injustice.

One way of dealing with these issues would be to add hidden social and environmental costs to all products. These presently give some countries an unfair trading advantage, especially those which allow businesses to damage the environment or exploit their workers. Unfortunately, external costs are hard to measure, and numerous opportunities exist for countries to manipulate their statistics.

Industrialization has created meager working conditions for children in some countries. For example, these boys in New Delhi, India, are carrying bricks to a construction site.

CITES

One of the best-known multilateral agreements affecting trade and the environment is the UN-sponsored Convention on International Trade in Endangered Species (CITES), agreed upon in 1973. CITES aims to prevent trade in rare animals and exotic products such as ivory, tiger bones, rhinoceros horns, and leopard skins. CITES is an important safeguard for the global wildlife trade, estimated to be worth billions. There is fierce argument between those who believe that carefully regulated trade in animal products can help to ensure the survival of endangered species and those who regard this as an unacceptable form of animal exploitation.

Unfortunately, international law cannot be enforced in the same way as domestic law, and countries cannot be compelled to perform their legal obligations. Although there is a procedure for going to court under international law, such cases are rare. International conventions obviously cannot be effective unless all the big trading nations take them seriously. Consumer awareness and environmental lobbies may be important factors in the industrialized world, but they carry little weight in most developing countries. So far, no trade dispute involving international environmental conventions has ever been taken to the GATT or the WTO, but trade disputes over national environmental measures are common.

Hundreds of thousands of elephants have been illegally killed by poachers. In 1989, CITES banned the trade of ivory and elephant products.

KEY CONCEPTS

Anti-globalist Anti-globalists and anti-global activists argue that world trade treaties benefit big corporations and rich countries at the expense of the environment and workers. At one end of the anti-globalist political spectrum are those who argue for strong national, ethnic, tribal, or religious identities, boundaries, and power. At the other end of the spectrum are those who are most concerned about the poor and powerless, and with protecting the environment.

Labor standards Labor standards are a set of government regulations designed to protect the rights of workers. Under such regulations, all companies must meet a set of standards that address the social and environmental well-being of all workers. Examples of labor standards include providing a safe and healthy workplace, preventing child labor, offering non-discrimination in employment, and ensuring a minimum wage is met.

Trading to a Better World?

The competitive international trading system has arguably driven down wages and destroyed the environment, or it has contributed to better living standards and improved environmental protection. Between 1820 and 1992, world population grew 5-fold, and world trade grew more than 500-fold. In the free trade decades of the 19th century, prosperity grew rapidly in newly industrialized countries. The pace of improvement declined when protectionist policies took hold and then took off again in the period from 1950 to 1970. During the period following the first GATT agreements, industrialized countries enjoyed a mixture of economic growth, full employment, low inflation, and growing international trade. The 1944 Bretton Woods Agreement created a new economic order, fostering a favorable environment for trade.

Market forces alone would be a politically dangerous and socially unacceptable approach to running the world. Yet market forces can provide the engine for both economic and social development. How can we ensure that an open global market does not result in such a competitive environment that wages and environmental health suffer? Unless quality of life

Working conditions in factories have improved. Today's factories are well lit and ventilated, and provide medical staff and cafeterias for their employees.

criteria such as working conditions, human rights, and environmental protection are built into the world trading system, the outlook is bleak for the future of human society. All the great civilizations have been built on trade, but trade alone did not sustain them.

With growing economic globalization guaranteed, the world must ensure:

1. that competitive trade does not destroy jobs and drive down wages and working conditions, increasing the gap between rich and poor;

2. that global trade does not harm the environment;

3. that trade in monetary products such as foreign exchange and financial derivatives does not destabilize the world trading system; and

4. that developing countries can be helped to improve living standards through the benefits of trade.

All of this argues for a strengthening of the WTO's political role in creating a new world economic order, along with the World Bank, the IMF, and other international institutions. International trade is certain to grow. Whether it helps or hinders the broader social and environmental objectives of global civilization will depend, to an important degree, on WTO policy. That policy depends in turn on the political will of member states.

NAFTA—AN IMPORTANT EXPERIMENT IN FREE TRADE

Some critics of free trade hold that the North American Free Trade Agreement (NAFTA) and liberalization led directly to the spectacular collapse of the Mexican economy at the end of 1994. Others point to the long period of protectionism that made Mexico's industries uncompetitive and its public sector too big of a drain on the budget. This perhaps over-ambitious move made by Mexico forced a rapid change from a closed economy to an open economy. At the same time, the country was moving from authoritarian one-party rule to democracy. Speculative money that had flowed into Mexico in anticipation of NAFTA benefits quickly evaporated as fear of political instability followed the assassination of the man expected to be Mexico's new president. It took a $50 billion international support package quickly arranged by the United States to restore confidence in the Mexican economy.

Membership in NAFTA helped the Mexican economy to grow at an adjusted annual rate of 2.3 percent between 1994 and 1999. During these years, inflation and unemployment fell, and the peso's value stabilized. In 2001, Mexico exported $139 billion to its NAFTA partners, an increase of 225 percent from 1993. Growth in Mexican imports accounted for more than half the increase in Mexico's gross domestic product during the period between 1993 and 2001.

Between 1994 and 2000, Mexico's average capital inflow reached $11.7 billion. This amount was three times what Mexico received during the seven years prior to the signing of NAFTA. Annual inflows to Canada between 1994 and 2000, meanwhile, averaged $21.4 billion, about four times the average in the seven years preceding the agreement. The United States also received large inflows of foreign capital during the same period. The fact that total trade between the U.S. and Mexico stood at $261 billion in 2000, three times the 1993 pre-NAFTA average, supports the agreement. The hope is that, in the long term, all three member countries of NAFTA will benefit from the increase in mutual trade. Criticism that NAFTA should have included stronger social and environmental programs has been partially offset by the member countries' signing two other agreements—the North American Agreement on Labor Cooperation and the North American Agreement on Environmental Cooperation.

Services are the largest and most dynamic component of the economies of both developed and developing countries. In addition to being important sources of revenue, they are also critical in the production of most goods. Service industries are engaged in the fields of financial services, including banking, computer services, distribution services, energy services, environmental services, express delivery, insurance, and telecommunications.

Though physical goods still account for 80 percent of global imports and exports, trade in services is growing fast. Service industries have replaced manufacturing as the main employers in the developed world. Liberalization of trade in services could lead to the export of jobs in these fields.

As an outcome of the Uruguay Round, trade in agricultural products was liberalized over the following decade so that farm goods could be traded almost as freely as manufactured goods. The poorest countries, however, were allowed to keep tariff barriers in place to protect their farming communities. Large-scale intensive farms able to produce cheap food were the major beneficiaries of global free trade in food. There is concern that farmers in the developing world will be driven to adopt these intensive farming methods in order to compete with the EU and the U.S., leaving uncertainty about the future of the traditional rural society.

Many Americans have become increasingly undecided about globalization. Although they support open markets in principle, they are also concerned with the impact of trade on the environment and working conditions. Some observers suspect that it may only be a matter of time before popular sentiment has a significant impact on U.S. trade policy. Some people have argued that democracy contributes to the problem because it typically puts national considerations such as job losses and corporate lobbying before the interests of the international community. This does not mean democracy is bad for the world. It means that finding solutions to global problems is a messy business. Without global bodies such as the WTO, it would certainly be impossible.

Fruit production plays a central role in world agriculture. Fruit has adapted to a wide range of climates and soils.

KEY CONCEPTS

Bretton Woods Agreement
The Bretton Woods Agreement established a post-war international monetary system of convertible currencies, fixed exchange rates, and free trade. The agreement established the IMF, the World Bank, and the International Trade Organization (ITO). It was negotiated in Bretton Woods, New Hampshire, in 1944.

Recognizing that the regulation of global trade is an ongoing process, in 2001, the United Nations Report of the High-Level Panel on Financing for Development urged that the WTO undertake a round of trade negotiations to fully bring developing countries into the global trading system. Specifically, the report says the WTO needs to fully implement the Uruguay commitments made by industrial countries, liberalize trade in agricultural products, reduce tariff peaks and tariff escalation, and reconsider trade-related intellectual property protection. The WTO must also provide for countries in the early stages of industrialization to appropriately protect their new industries, consider possible rules governing the temporary movement of labor, and eliminate remaining trade barriers in manufacturing and services. The report went on to recommend that the least developed countries be given immediate financial assistance to help them improve their position in the world trading system.

Cattle are often raised for their meat and milk. They are sometimes used to pull carts, plows, and wagons. In some parts of the world, a family's wealth is judged by the number of cattle it owns.

Time Line of Events

138 B.C.

A Chinese expedition led by Zhang Qian, the father of the Silk Road, opens a trade route to the West.

A.D. 1500

European trade empires begin to form.

1600s

The East India Company is established in England.

1776

Adam Smith's *The Wealth of Nations* is published. The five-volume work stresses the benefits of division of labor or specialization and outlines the workings of the price system.

1829

Jean Baptiste Say's *Cours Complet d'Économie Politique Pratique* is published. Say, a proponent of laissez-faire policies, the idea that government does not become involved in business, introduces Adam Smith's work to continental Europe.

1936

John Maynard Keynes's *The General Theory of Employment, Interest and Money* is published. This work is considered to be the first text of modern macroeconomics, the study of controlling factors in the economy as a whole.

1947

The General Agreement on Tariffs and Trade (GATT) becomes the agreement and organization for establishing and enforcing international trade rules through dispute settlement.

1957

The Treaty of Rome is signed by West Germany, France, Italy, the Netherlands, Belgium, and Luxembourg, establishing a trading bloc.

1960s

The integrated global capital market and large-scale global interdependence begin.

Early 1970s

Japan and the Soviet Union are transformed from exporters to major importers.

1976

Economist Milton Friedman wins the Nobel Prize for Economics.

Mid-1980s

United States President Ronald Reagan and British Prime Minister Margaret Thatcher promote pervasive non-tariff barriers and trade liberalization policies. The number of transnational corporations (TNCs) rises.

1986

The Uruguay Round of GATT commences.

1989

The Canada–U.S. Free Trade Agreement (CFTA) is signed as a precursor to the North American Free Trade Agreement (NAFTA).

1994

The Eighth (Uruguay) Round of GATT establishes the World Trade Organization (WTO).

1994

NAFTA becomes effective.

1995

In January, the GATT agreement on trade in goods officially becomes the WTO.

1996

The first WTO Ministerial Conference takes place in December in Singapore. Meetings examine issues related to the work of the WTO's first two years of activity and the implementation of the Uruguay Round Agreements.

1997

More than 50 WTO members agree to eliminate customs duties and other duties and charges on information technology products by the year 2000. Duties and charges are also eliminated on trade in banking, insurance, securities, and financial information.

1997

An agreement to expand trade in basic telecommunications is reached in February.

1998

The second WTO Ministerial Conference is held in Geneva, Switzerland. Ministers pave the way for negotiations that could lead to further liberalization.

Softwood lumber is often used in home construction. The United States imposed tariffs on Canadian softwood lumber imports in 2002.

1999

The third WTO Ministerial Conference is held in Seattle, Washington, in November. Talks at the WTO are suspended. Anti-globalists protest the conference, claiming the WTO represents elite interests that fail to protect the environment and ensure social justice.

2001

The fourth WTO Ministerial Conference is held in Doha, Qatar. Ministers agree to start negotiations on specific issues relating to trade and environment.

2002

The WTO's Dispute Settlement Body establishes panels to examine the equalizing tax Florida has imposed on processed oranges and grapefruit, and U.S. duties on softwood lumber imports from Canada.

Concept Web

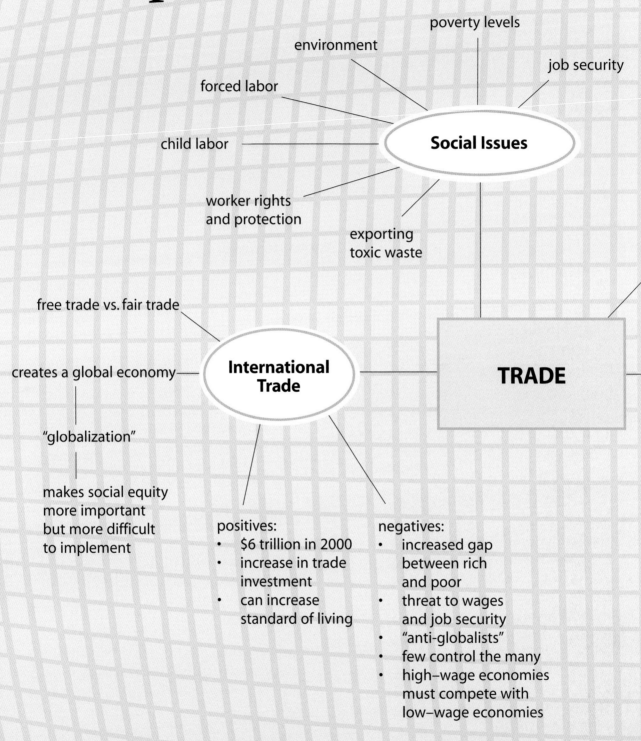

poverty levels

environment

job security

forced labor

Social Issues

child labor

worker rights
and protection

exporting
toxic waste

free trade vs. fair trade

**International
Trade**

TRADE

creates a global economy

"globalization"

makes social equity
more important
but more difficult
to implement

positives:
- $6 trillion in 2000
- increase in trade
  investment
- can increase
  standard of living

negatives:
- increased gap
  between rich
  and poor
- threat to wages
  and job security
- "anti-globalists"
- few control the many
- high–wage economies
  must compete with
  low–wage economies

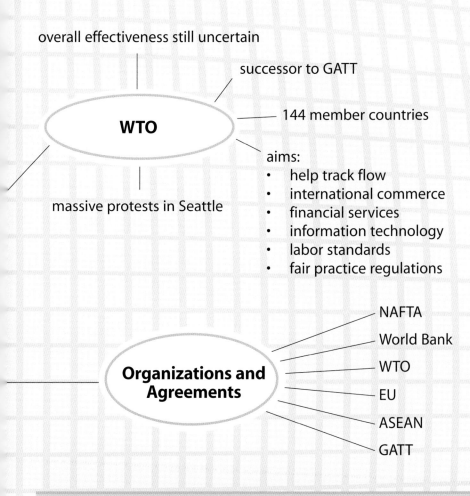

overall effectiveness still uncertain

successor to GATT

WTO

144 member countries

massive protests in Seattle

aims:
- help track flow
- international commerce
- financial services
- information technology
- labor standards
- fair practice regulations

Organizations and Agreements

NAFTA

World Bank

WTO

EU

ASEAN

GATT

MAKE YOUR OWN CONCEPT WEB

A concept web is a useful summary tool. It can also be used to plan your research or help you write an essay or report. To make your own concept map, follow the steps below:

- You will need a large piece of unlined paper and a pencil.
- First, read through your source material, such as *The Globalization of Trade* in the Understanding Global Issues series.
- Write the main idea, or concept, in large letters in the center of the page.
- On a sheet of lined paper, jot down all words, phrases, or lists that you know are connected with the concept. Try to do this from memory.
- Look at your list. Can you group your words and phrases in certain topics or themes? Connect the different topics with lines to the center, or to other "branches."
- Critique your concept web. Ask questions about the material on your concept web: Does it all make sense? Are all the links shown? Could there be other ways of looking at it? Is anything missing?
- What more do you need to find out? Develop questions for those areas you are still unsure about or where information is missing. Use these questions as a basis for further research.

Quiz

Multiple Choice

1. The World Trade Organization (WTO) was established to:
   a) standardize world currency
   b) promote open, fair, and undistorted competition in world commerce
   c) protect the environment
   d) all of the above

2. The WTO grew out of:
   a) the General Agreement on Tariffs and Trade (GATT)
   b) the Organization for Economic Co-operation and Development (OECD)
   c) the North American Free Trade Agreement (NAFTA)
   d) the European Union (EU)

3. How many countries belong to the WTO?
   a) 115
   b) 144
   c) 184
   d) 27

4. In what year did the WTO come into being?
   a) 1947
   b) 1994
   c) 1995
   d) 1998

5. Trade disputes among WTO-member countries are settled by:
   a) the International Court of Justice
   b) the WTO's General Council
   c) the WTO secretariat
   d) the United Nations

6. The WTO can enforce its decisions:
   a) only if member countries agree to abide by them
   b) by calling on United Nations peacekeeping forces
   c) by asking the United States to intervene
   d) never

7. The 1999 WTO Ministerial Conference in Seattle made worldwide headlines because:
   a) China was admitted to the WTO
   b) the United States walked out
   c) anti-globalist protesters wreaked havoc in the streets
   d) all of the above

Name the Location

1. The WTO's headquarters
2. The Mercosur free trade area
3. The ASEAN free trade area

True or False

1. Almost half of the world's population lives on less than $2 per day.
2. New WTO members are required to abide by all of the provisions under the WTO's rules of membership.
3. Under WTO rules, the poorest countries are granted special trade access conditions.
4. The North American Free Trade Agreement (NAFTA) links the economies of the United States, Canada, and Mexico.

Answers on page 53

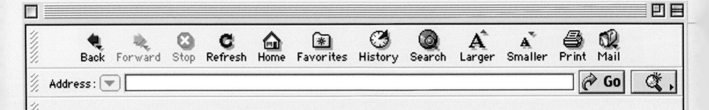

Internet Resources

The following Web sites provide more information on global trade:

WTO

http://www.wto.org

The WTO Web site provides news and information about the World Trade Organization, including the body's decisions and ongoing negotiations. The site includes background information, trade topics, resources, documents, and forums.

USTR

http://www.ustr.gov

The USTR Web site is the official Internet site of the Office of the United States Trade Representative. The main page links to a separate WTO & Multilateral Affairs page that describes some of the trade agreements that the United States is party to. The page dedicated to the WTO includes extensive information about the trade organization, and its relations with the United States and other members.

Some Web sites stay current longer than others. To find other global trade Web sites, enter terms such as "tariff," "free trade," or "globalization" into a search engine.

Further Reading

Aaronson, Susan Ariel. *Taking Trade to the Streets: The Lost History of Public Efforts to Shape Globalization.* Ann Arbor, MI: University of Michigan, 2001.

Burgess, John. *World Trade.* Broomall, PA: Chelsea House Publishers, 2001.

Gilpin, Robert, and Jean M. Gilpin. *Global Political Economy: Understanding the International Economic Order.* Princeton, NJ: Princeton University Press, 2001.

Gray, John. *False Dawn: The Delusions of Global Capitalism.* New York: New Press, 2000.

Moore, Mike. *A World Without Walls: Freedom, Development, Free Trade and Global Governance.* Cambridge, UK: Cambridge University Press, 2003.

Singer, Peter. *One World: The Ethics of Globalization.* New Haven, CT: Yale University Press, 2002.

Smith, Adam. *The Wealth of Nations.* Amherst, NY: Prometheus Books, 1991.

Soros, George. *George Soros on Globalization.* New York: George Soros Public Affairs, 2002.

Answers

MULTIPLE CHOICE
  1. b) 2. a) 3. b) 4. c) 5. b) 6. a) 7. c)

NAME THE LOCATION
  1. Geneva, Switzerland
  2. South America
  3. Southeast Asia

TRUE OR FALSE
  1. T 2. T 3. T 4. T

Glossary

anarchy: a state of society without government or law

bilateral: pertaining to two countries

consensus: a decision reached by a group as a whole

developed countries: countries in the industrialized world; highly economically and technologically developed

developing countries: those countries that are undergoing the process of industrialization, sometimes collectively referred to as the "Third World"

economic restructuring: affecting a fundamental change in the use of wealth, income, and commodities

fair trade: trade aimed at achieving sustainable development for excluded and disadvantaged producers

foreign direct investment (FDI): a partnership between a transnational company (TNC) and a foreign company

free trade: trade in which governments do not interfere or regulate international business with tariffs

globalization: the increased mobility of goods, services, labor, technology, and capital throughout the world

gross domestic product (GDP): the market value of all goods and services produced in a year within a country's borders

information technology: all forms of technology used to create, store, exchange, and use information in its various forms

intellectual property: any product of the human intellect that is unique, novel, and not obvious

multilateral: pertaining to multiple countries; in the context of the WTO, multilateral agreements are distinguished from more limited, regional agreements

plurilateral: pertaining to a few countries

protectionism: a government's placing of duties or quotas on imports to protect domestic industries from global competition

subsidies: financial aid given by a government to individuals or groups

transparency: a controversial term for ensuring that reported financial data reflects reality; full transparency requires that changes in financial status of a reporting entity be reflected instantaneously to all concerned

World Bank: owned by 184 countries, it consists of five institutions that work toward poverty reduction and improving standards of living for people in the developing world

Index

activists 26, 27, 41
anti-globalists 5, 41, 47, 48
anti-globalization 5, 26, 27

Bretton Woods agreement 42, 44

Cold War 12, 13
Convention on International Trade in
    Endangered Species of Wild Fauna and
    Flora (CITES) 41

economists 7, 11, 15, 36, 46, 47
environment 7, 8, 9, 10, 13, 14, 24, 25, 27, 28,
    35, 38, 39, 40, 41, 42, 43, 44, 47, 48
European Union (EU) 19, 20, 22, 25, 27, 28, 33,
    44, 49
exports 6, 11, 16, 19, 21, 25, 27, 32, 33, 37, 39,
    43, 44, 46, 48

foreign direct investment (FDI) 7, 22, 24, 27
free market 6, 13, 21, 27, 28, 29, 34, 36
free trade 5, 7, 10, 13, 24, 25, 27, 29, 34, 36, 37,
    38, 39, 42, 43, 44, 46, 48

General Agreement on Tariffs and Trade
    (GATT) 5, 8, 12, 13, 15, 16, 19, 20, 35, 36,
    40, 41, 42, 46, 47, 49
globalization 5, 24, 25, 26, 27, 28, 39, 43, 44, 48,
    49

imports 10, 11, 16, 19, 20, 21, 25, 32, 33, 35, 36,
    40, 43, 44, 46, 47
International Monetary Fund (IMF) 12, 16, 19,
    43, 44

lobbying 20, 23, 26, 44

Mexico 7, 10, 25, 26, 27, 28, 33, 38, 40, 43

North American Free Trade Agreement
    (NAFTA) 7, 10, 25, 26, 27, 28, 43, 46, 49

Organization for Economic Co-operation and
    Development (OECD) 5, 36

Panitchpakdi, Supachai Dr. 15, 17

Ruggiero, Renato 15

Seattle, Washington 5, 38, 47, 49
Smith, Adam 29, 46

tariffs 5, 10, 13, 14, 16, 18, 28, 29, 36, 37, 44, 45,
    46, 47
trade disputes 8, 18, 19, 41, 46, 47
trading blocs 14, 25, 28, 46

United Nations (UN) 12, 13, 26, 41, 45
United States (U.S.) 5, 10, 11, 12, 15, 16, 19, 20,
    21, 24, 25, 26, 27, 28, 33, 35, 39, 40, 43, 44,
    46, 47
Uruguay Round 13, 15, 16, 17, 36, 37, 44, 45,
    46, 47

World Bank 12, 19, 36, 43, 44, 49
World Trade Organization (WTO) 5, 8, 9, 12,
    13, 14, 15, 16, 17, 18, 19, 20, 21, 22, 24, 25,
    26, 28, 30, 35, 36, 38, 39, 40, 41, 43, 44, 45,
    46, 47, 49
World War II 5, 12, 13

Photo Credits